Under Wraps

The Gift We Never Expected

Leader Guide

Under Wraps
The Gift We Never Expected

Book
978-1-4267-9373-8
978-1-6308-8296-9 (Large Print)
Also available as an eBook

Leader Guide
978-1-4267-9375-2
Also available as an eBook

DVD
978-1-4267-9378-3

Devotional
978-1-4267-9376-9
Also available as an eBook

Children's Leader Guide
978-1-4267-9381-3

Youth Study Book
978-1-4267-9379-0
Also available as an eBook

Worship Planning
978-1-4267-9382-0 (Flash Drive)
978-1-6308-8069-9 (Download)

Under Wraps

The Gift We Never Expected

Jessica LaGrone
Andy Nixon
Rob Renfroe
Ed Robb

Leader Guide
Jenny Youngman

Abingdon Press
Nashville

UNDER WRAPS:
THE GIFT WE NEVER EXPECTED - LEADER GUIDE

This book is printed on elemental, chlorine-free paper

ISBN 978-1-4267-9375-2

14 15 16 17 18 19 20 21 22 23—10 9 8 7 6 5 4 3 2 1

MANUFACTURED IN THE UNITED STATES OF AMERICA

Contents

Introduction

The season of Advent—the four Sundays leading up to Christmas Day—is a special time for believers. It challenges us to pause and remember the hope we have during a stressful season that all too often emphasizes greed and money. Advent allows us the time and space to refocus our hearts and minds on Jesus—the true hope of the season. The observation of Advent is a gift, a time to reflect, meditate, and pray, asking God to do a great work in our hearts as we remember anew the great gift given to us through his Son. We observe Advent because God expects something amazing to happen in our lives at Christmas.

The theme of *Under Wraps* reflects how the character of God, communicated through the Old Testament, is revealed completely and perfectly in Jesus. Together we will see specifically how four characteristics of God . . .

God is expectant;
God is dangerous;
God is jealous;
God is faithful;

are described in the Old Testament and then revealed through Jesus and the time he spent here on earth.

Jesus—God under wraps—took on human flesh and came to live among us to show us who God is and what he is like. And he came on a mission—to rescue us and redeem us so that we could fully know God and be known by him.

About the Book for Group Members

Before the first session, you will want to distribute copies of the *Under Wraps* book to the members of your group. Be sure to communicate that they are to read the Introduction and Chapter 1 *before* your first group session.

About This Leader Guide

As you gather each week with the members of your group, you will have the opportunity to watch a video, discuss and respond to what you're learning, and pray together. You will need access to a television and DVD player with working remotes.

To create a warm and inviting atmosphere for your group sessions and to connect with the study's theme of God "under wraps," you might consider displaying a small artificial Christmas tree with some pretty wrapped packages underneath—or simply one package wrapped in red paper and a bow. Though optional, you also might consider serving Christmas cookies as refreshments.

This leader guide and the DVD will be your primary tools for leading each group session. In this book you will find outlines for four group sessions and a bonus Christmas session, each formatted for a 60-minute session. (For a 90-minute session, extend the discussion and prayer time.) Each session plan follows this format:

Preparation (Before the Session)

For your preparation prior to the group session, this section provides a clear objective for the session, the main themes of the chapter, a key Scripture, and a list of materials and equipment needed. Be sure to read this section, as well as the session outline, before the group gathers. If you choose, you also may find it helpful to review the DVD segment in advance.

Getting Started (10 minutes)

Begin every session with an *Opening Prayer*. You may want to pray your own prayer or invite participants to pray. Or if you prefer, you may use the printed opening prayer provided in every session. After the prayer, there is a *Conversation Starter* and some discussion questions. Feel free to choose one of these, putting it into your own words.

Video, Discussion, and Application (40 minutes)

Once you have introduced the topic and settled into the gathering, watch the week's video segment together. When the video is over, discuss the questions that cover material from *The Video* and *The Book*. Then you'll find instructions for a brief *Bible Study* on some of the Scriptures from the chapter.

After *Bible Study* comes *Life Application*. Spend some time here considering what all the material and Scriptures mean for your daily lives. Each week you'll encourage participants to complete an exercise to help them put their learnings into practice.

Closing (10 minutes)

Each session closes with some thoughts from the chapter for you to read aloud. Finally, you'll close in prayer—using either the printed prayer or saying one of your own.

Before You Begin

It has been said that there are three keys to a successful study: 1) prayer, 2) preparation, and 3) personalization. Pray for each and every member of your group by name, pray for each session, and pray for God to use you as his instrument. Do your homework by reading the chapters and preparing for each session well in advance of your meeting time. And finally, personalize the study. You are encouraged to modify or adapt the session outlines and activities to match your teaching style and/or to meet the needs and interests of your group.

May God richly bless your time together as you unwrap the gift he has for you in Jesus Christ!

Session 1
God Is Expectant

Session 1

God Is Expectant

Preparation

Session Objective

Participants will reflect upon God as an eager Gift-giver who expects to break through to the world, bringing hope to the darkest places and forever changing our understanding of God's love and grace.

Main Themes

- Mary and Elizabeth were unlikely choices for lead characters in the Nativity story, but these expectant mothers said an obedient yes to God's invitation to tell God's great love story.

- God's people had waited for a Messiah for generations, but the arrival of Jesus was not what they expected. They had to adjust their expectations and let God's story unfold.
- God loves us with an expectant heart and is eager to lavish gifts upon us.

Key Scripture

All this took place to fulfill what the Lord had said through the prophet: "The virgin will conceive and give birth to a son, and they will call him Immanuel" (which means "God with us").

Matthew 1:22-23

Materials Needed

You will need the *Under Wraps DVD*, a DVD player, and a Bible.

Getting Started (10 Minutes)

Opening Prayer

Loving God, we are so grateful that you stepped down into our time and space to show us that you are love and light and hope and joy and peace. We thank you for loving us so perfectly well. Fill us with your presence as we immerse ourselves back into your amazing, world-changing story. Give us hearts to expect that you will work and move in us this holy season. In Jesus' name. Amen.

Conversation Starter

Say:

This week we read about the expectant nature of God, full of hope and eagerness to give good gifts to God's children. Today we will discuss and reflect upon God's eagerness to surprise us, and invite God to give us expectant hearts to receive his gifts.

Ask:

Choose one of the following:

- When have you been so excited to give a gift that you could hardly contain your excitement?
- Have you ever considered that God is expectant and eager to surprise you? How would you describe the idea that God is expectant?
- How have you received surprising gifts from God?

Video, Discussion, and Application (40 Minutes)

Note: This section allows approximately 25 minutes total for discussion (of video, Scriptures, and book). More questions are provided than you will have time to cover; select in advance those questions you would like to discuss, putting a checkmark beside each one.

The Video

Play: Session 1: God Is Expectant (running time: 13:45)

Discuss:

- What is significant about the relationship and the conditions of Mary and Elizabeth?
- What kind of Messiah were God's people looking for? How was Jesus different from those expectations?
- How was God described as expectant in the video?
- In an instant-gratification kind of world, how does Advent teach us to wait? Why is waiting good for us?
- What does God expect to happen at Christmas?
- What do you expect to happen at Christmas?

The Book

In Chapter 1, we discovered that we all have different expectations about what Christmas brings. Elizabeth, Mary, and even God himself had expectations for that first Christmas. God expected to change the world and to breathe new life into even the hardest of hearts.

Discuss:

- Why does Christmas bring with it so many expectations?

- Mary was pregnant unexpectedly because of her young age and unwed status. Elizabeth was pregnant unexpectedly because of her old age. How do these unexpected circumstances set the stage for even more unexpected details about the Messiah that were still to come?
- Name some of the ways that Jesus defied expectations from the very beginning of his life all the way to the end.
- Reflect on the idea that God is like an eager Gift-giver. He has the perfect gift for you and can't wait until it's time to give it you. How do you receive his gift at Christmas? How do you receive it throughout the year?
- Jessica wrote about "we" language her community used when she was pregnant with her first child. Why do you think we use "we" language when it comes to the arrival of new babies? What is significant about "we" language surrounding the birth of Jesus?
- Review the story of the farmer who refused to go to church and came to believe in Jesus after attempting to rescue a flock of birds. Who are some "farmers" in your life that need the gift of Jesus Christ in their lives? Who does your heart break for? Who do you want God to get through to this Christmas?

Bible Study

In Advance: Use a commentary or Bible dictionary as needed to help you prepare for this segment. Choose one or more of the following texts (depending upon time available and your group dynamics and needs). Be familiar with the text before the group session begins. Write down your own discussion questions in addition to those provided below.

Read Aloud: Isaiah 9:6-7

Discuss:

- How is the Messiah described in this passage?
- If you didn't know the full story of Jesus and you heard this passage, how would you have thought this Messiah would come into the world?
- How was Jesus an unexpected fulfillment of this prophecy?

Read Aloud: John 1:14

Discuss:

- Review the section in Chapter 1 about the Greek word for dwelling. What does it mean that God put on flesh?
- What is the significance of Jesus putting on our "tent" and moving into our "camp"?

Read Aloud: Luke 1:46-55

Discuss:

- What is unexpected about Mary's declarations?

- Mary mentions God's promises to Abraham. How would God's people, who had heard about these promises for generations, have been surprised at what the fulfillment of the promise looked like?
- Mary's song comes before she ever holds Jesus in her arms. With the child in her womb, she believes with all confidence in the fulfillment of God's promise and gives new imagery for what God has done by sending Jesus to live among us. What does she proclaim that God has done?

Conclude by reading Isaiah 25:6, 8-9 aloud. Remind participants that Christmas is a celebration of Jesus; and while Advent can feel more like a season of hurry-up-and-get-ready-for-Christmas, Advent is meant to cause us to slow down, to wait, and to seek God—to look for the coming Light. As preparing for Christmas fills up our calendars, let's redirect our hearts and minds to this truth: "This is the Lord for whom we have waited; let us be glad and rejoice in his salvation."

Life Application

Say:

We talked earlier about people in our lives who need to receive the gift of Jesus. Maybe you are the one who needs to receive the gift of Jesus, whether for the first time or as a renewed experience of his grace. Remember this: God expected to change the world through the birth of his Son. God expected to break through to bring hope and joy and peace and light. God expected to see hardened hearts soften and turn to him.

You are invited to examine your state of need before God. This week, spend time in prayer each day asking God for a renewed and fresh experience of the gift of Jesus in your life. Ask God to break through to your heart in ways that you have not yet known.

Then, invite God to give you awareness of those people in your life who do not know Jesus. Pray for the diligence to pray for these people and for the courage to invite them to church or to tell them the story of Jesus.

This week be on the lookout for new ways that God is breaking through to your heart or showing you how to reach out to someone who hasn't yet received the gift of Jesus.

Closing (10 Minutes)

A Final Reflection

Say:

What are you expecting this Christmas? Do you have a longing that God will change something in our world? That God will change someone you love? That God will change *you*? God loves an expectant heart, and he is eager to surprise us with the gifts of his goodness and love. May we wait for him with eager hearts.

Closing Prayer

Loving God, we are so grateful for your extravagant gift of love, your only Son, coming into our lives. We are grateful that you expected to change the world and to break through to even the hardest of hearts, including our own. Help us to expect life change. Help us to expect peace. Help us to expect joy. Help us to expect hope. We seek you and we wait this Advent. Amen.

Session 2

God Is Dangerous

Session 2

God Is Dangerous

Preparation

Session Objective

Participants will discover that God is mighty and has powerful plans for his children. God so loved the world that he calls us to live our lives to the fullest, which sometimes means we are called to tasks we never imagined ourselves undertaking, challenges we feel ill equipped to handle, and unknown territory where we may not want to go.

Main Themes

- Jesus was born into a dangerous situation, as King Herod felt threatened by a new baby king having been born.

- Life with God is dangerous because he wants more for us than we've considered and has bolder dreams for us than we've dreamed.
- God wants us to have a dangerous faith—one that loves with abandon and is focused on the mission of Jesus Christ in the world.

Key Scripture

For God so loved the world that he gave his one and only Son, that whoever believes in him shall not perish but have eternal life. For God did not send his Son into the world to condemn the world, but to save the world through him.

John 3:16-17

Materials Needed

You will need the *Under Wraps DVD*, a DVD player, and a Bible.

Getting Started (10 Minutes)

Opening Prayer

Loving God, you are dangerous, but you are good. You don't call us to safety but to live out your story in our lives with bravery and trust in your faithfulness. Thank you for stepping down into our world to save us and to love us. Give us wisdom now as we study your Word. Amen.

Conversation Starter

Say:

This week we read about the ways in which a life with God can be dangerous. Today we will discuss and reflect upon God's call in our lives to live out Jesus' mission in the world—even if it isn't always the safest path.

Ask:

Choose one of the following:

- What is the most dangerous situation you have ever faced?
- What do you think of when you reflect on the idea of God as dangerous?
- Have you ever sensed God calling you out of your comfort zone? When?

Video, Discussion, and Application (40 Minutes)

Note: This section allows approximately 25 minutes total for discussion (of video, Scriptures, and book). More questions are provided than you will have time to cover; select in advance those questions you would like to discuss, putting a checkmark beside each one.

The Video

Play: Session 2: God Is Dangerous (running time: 16:40)

Discuss:

- Why is it surprising to consider that Jesus' coming would be dangerous?
- What is the "cosmic struggle" referred to? How is this dangerous to the world?
- Jesus came to destroy the works of the devil. How is this a dangerous mission?
- Why was Herod troubled at news of the birth of Jesus?
- How did Jesus challenge the reign of corruption in his day?
- How is a life of following after God dangerous?

The Book

In Chapter 2, we discovered that even in his infancy, Jesus was dangerous. He was dangerous to the government, he was dangerous for Mary and Joseph, and his mission would be dangerous for his followers as they would be called to take his light to the darkest corners of the world.

Discuss:

- What words come to mind when you think about a newborn baby? Why is *dangerous* not a word we typically connect with babies? How does this word apply to the Christ child?

- What are some examples from the Bible of the dangerous nature of God?
- When God calls people to dangerous situations, what does he always provide?
- Jesus' birth shook up the powers of the world in many ways. Name some of the ways mentioned in Chapter 2.
- Read aloud the following statement: "An encounter with Jesus is always dangerous because he has big things in mind for us, and it's probably going to be more than we ever dreamed of or expected." How have you found this to be true in your own life?
- Review the details of Dietrich Bonhoeffer's life. What are some other examples of people who walked into dangerous territory for the sake of the gospel?

Bible Study

In Advance: Use a commentary or Bible dictionary as needed to help you prepare for this segment. Choose one or more of the following texts (depending upon time available and your group dynamics and needs). Be familiar with the text before the group session begins. Write down your own discussion questions in addition to those provided below.

Read Aloud: Matthew 10:34-42

Discuss:

- What is Jesus referring to in these verses?
- How does this passage demonstrate the danger of following Jesus?
- What does it cost to follow Jesus?
- What is dangerous about losing our life and finding it again in Jesus?

Read Aloud: Ephesians 6:10-20

Discuss:

- Review the section in Chapter 2 about the spiritual forces of darkness. Why did Jesus need to come to overthrow these forces of darkness?
- What are the dangers of the world? How does Jesus' coming undo the powers of evil in the world?
- How does the "armor of God" protect us from the danger of evil?

Read Aloud: John 17:15-17

Discuss:

- What is Jesus' prayer for his followers?
- Jesus knew that the world would be a dangerous place for his followers. How does he equip us for the mission?

Conclude by reading John 3:16-19, 36 aloud. Remind participants that even though we celebrate with joy at Christmas, we
should also remember that the sweet baby in the manger came
to overcome evil and injustice in the world and to do a work in
us, making us holy as he is holy.

Life Application

Say:

We have explored some ways that Jesus is dangerous to the
powers of the world and touched on some ways that following
Jesus can be dangerous. In Chapter 2 we read these words:
"God's work in our lives doesn't always feel comfortable.
Sometimes it doesn't make sense. Sometimes it hurts. Why
put you through these renovations? Because God intends to
come and reside there. That's what he's doing in our lives. The
King wants to move in. And he's got work to do." It can be a
dangerous task to let God into your heart so that he can clear
out the things that take up too much space, tear down walls,
and lead a renovation and restoration project in you.

So this week, we are invited to ask God to put on his contractor
hat and do some demo. Spend time in prayer each day asking
God to expose things that you've kept from him. Though it
feels dangerous, be vulnerable before God and accept the gift
of his grace, mercy, forgiveness, and power to carry his light
to the world.

Closing (10 Minutes)

A Final Reflection

Say:

Do you have a dangerous faith, one that isn't afraid to follow the mission that is laid out before you no matter the cost or where it may take you? Is God calling you to leave your comfort zone and invite a neighbor to church or to a Bible study? Is God calling you to take a leap of faith and give sacrificially to your church in order to grow its outreach to your community? Is God calling you to trust in the gifts he has given you to be a voice of hope and faith in your local schools, your community, or your home? Is God calling you to stand above the culture and raise your voice against an injustice like human trafficking? Is God calling you to come face to face with the need in your area: to minister to those who are homeless, to open your heart and home to a child in the foster care system, or to mentor a youth who doesn't have a father? Is God calling you to face the unknown and offer yourself as a light into the world on a mission trip to Guatemala, India, or China? Following a mighty God like ours can be dangerous.

Jesus came to do a dangerous work in the world—to destroy the power of death and sin and restore us into a right relationship with himself. His message is not safe; his love for us is undaunted. He was not afraid to walk into the dark crevices of this world with his light. He fights for our hearts with his extraordinary love, and his sacrifice leads our hearts to say, "Yes, Lord, we will follow."

Closing Prayer

Mighty God, we thank you for breaking into our world to bring down systems of injustice and to bring your reign of peace, grace, and hope. Help us to boldly follow you and go where you send us to be your hands and feet in this world. As we wait in this season, work on our hearts, making them your home. Amen.

God Is Jealous

Session 3
God Is Jealous

Preparation

Session Objective

Participants will remember that God wants to be our first love and have first place in our lives. God is jealous for us and wants us to be completely available for Jesus to work in us—with nothing standing in the way.

Main Themes

- We are prone to wander away from God toward the idols of this world.
- God is jealous for our love.
- God wants us to be available for Jesus to work in us.

Key Scripture

He answered, "'Love the Lord your God with all your heart and with all your soul and with all your strength and with all your mind'; and, 'Love your neighbor as yourself.'"

Luke 10:27

Materials Needed

You will need the *Under Wraps DVD*, a DVD player, paper and pens for participants, and a Bible.

Getting Started (10 Minutes)

Opening Prayer

Loving God, thank you for loving us so much that you are jealous for our hearts. We confess that we often chase after lesser things in this world instead of giving ourselves fully to you. Forgive us and return us to our first love—you. Move in our hearts now as we study your word. Amen.

Conversation Starter

Say:

So far we have discovered that God is expectant, and we've read about the ways in which a life with God can be dangerous. Today we will be exploring the jealous nature of God and the commandment to put God first in our lives.

Ask:

Choose one of the following:

- What are some everyday or common examples of jealousy?
- What are some modern-day examples of idols?
- Why do you think God is jealous for us?

Video, Discussion, and Application (40 Minutes)

Note: This section allows approximately 25 minutes total for discussion (of video, Scriptures, and book). More questions are provided than you will have time to cover; select in advance those questions you would like to discuss, putting a checkmark beside each one.

The Video

Play: Session 3: God Is Jealous (running time: 15:35)

Discuss:

- How do we get the Christmas celebration wrong in our culture?
- How can our Christmas celebrations make God jealous?
- What does the Bible mean when it tells us that God is jealous?

- What are some ways that we can tangibly put Jesus first?
- Why do you think we sometimes dismiss nudges from the Holy Spirit?
- What happens when we listen to those nudges, when we love God and neighbor first?

The Book

In Chapter 3 we discovered that God is jealous for our hearts. He wants to be number one in our lives and in our hearts. We get Christmas and everything else wrong when we put anything ahead of God on our list of priorities.

Discuss:

- Why do you think Christmas in our culture has become mostly about the gifts?
- How can we celebrate Christmas, including the giving of gifts, and still keep God first?
- The Hebrew word for jealous means "warmth" or "heat" and describes an intensity and passion. How do these words help us understand what it means to say that God is jealous?
- What do we human beings do to make God jealous for our hearts?
- What is the way we live out Jesus' command to love God and love our neighbors?
- What are some ways that we can intentionally connect with God?

Bible Study

In Advance: Use a commentary or Bible dictionary as needed to help you prepare for this segment. Choose one or more of the following texts (depending upon time available and your group dynamics and needs). Be familiar with the text before the group session begins. Write down your own discussion questions in addition to those provided below.

Read Aloud: Deuteronomy 4:15-24

Discuss:

- List together all the things that Moses says not to make an idol of.
- Why do the Israelites need this warning?
- How is God all-consuming, jealous, or passionate?

Read Aloud: Deuteronomy 6:1-15

Discuss:

- What place does God want in our lives?
- What do these verses tell us about keeping God first in our families and communities?
- How do we sometimes forget God? What can we do to remember God and keep him first?

Read Aloud: Matthew 6:25, 32-33

Discuss:

- What does it mean to seek God's kingdom first?
- What other things do we seek in this world?
- What can we do to actively seek God first?

Conclude by reading Luke 10:27 aloud. Encourage participants by affirming that we all are guilty of putting other things before God at various times in our lives. As we prepare for Christmas this year, we can be sure to put God first by making ourselves completely available to Jesus.

Life Application

Say:

As we make ourselves available to Jesus this Advent, let's take a minute to make a list of our current priorities and to-dos. No one is going to look at this; we're not going to share what we write. This is just an exercise to see where God is on your Christmas list this year. *(Pause and allow participants to write their lists.)*

When you have your list, reflect on some intentional steps you can take to put God first or keep God first above every other thing in your life. *(Pause again, allowing participants a moment to reflect.)*

The Reflect section of Chapter 3 offers these questions for us as we close this week:

- How does it make you feel to know that God is jealous for your heart? Have you ever considered that before? Do you feel God speaking to you about any areas where you might have put something or someone ahead of him?
- Advent urges us to stop and remember God's great love for us and to reevaluate what place Jesus holds in our lives and our priorities. What would it be like to go through this season with God in first place? How could that change you? How could that change your family and the way you celebrate the season together?

Closing (10 Minutes)

A Final Reflection

Say:

As you put God first in your life, remember to invite God to give you awareness of those people in your life who do not know Jesus. Ask God for the diligence to pray for these people and for the courage to invite them to church or tell them the story of Jesus.

In our next session, be prepared to share a word or two about ways that you have made yourself more available to Jesus.

Closing Prayer

God of Love and Grace, we thank you for loving us so much that you are jealous for our hearts. Help us to put you first. Help us to make ourselves completely available to you. Come and make our hearts your home. Amen.

SESSION 4
God Is Faithful

SESSION 4
God Is Faithful

Preparation

Session Objective

Participants will discover that God's motivation and message in sending Jesus from the cradle to the cross was God's love for every person on earth.

Main Themes

- Amid life's challenges, we can be sure that God is both loving and faithful.
- A covenant is much more than a contract agreement; it is a vow to fulfill the promise even if the other person is unfaithful.

- Jesus was born to be our Savior because we desperately need one. He is the *why* of Christmas.

Key Scripture

See what great love the Father has lavished on us, that we should be called children of God! And that is what we are!

1 John 3:1

Materials Needed

You will need the *Under Wraps DVD*, a DVD player, paper and pens for participants, and a Bible.

Getting Started (10 Minutes)

Opening Prayer

Faithful God, to generations of wayward followers, you have always been faithful. You are faithful still. Thank you for Christmas. Thank you for fulfilling your covenant. Show us more of who you are as we study your word together. Amen.

Conversation Starter

Say:

So far we have discovered that God is expectant, dangerous, and jealous. Today we will be exploring God's promise to be faithful to us always.

Ask:

Choose one of the following:

- How would you explain the difference between a covenant and a contract?
- Other than God, who has been the most faithful person in your life? In what ways?
- What are some times that God has been especially faithful to you?

Video, Discussion, and Application (40 Minutes)

Note: This section allows approximately 25 minutes total for discussion (of video, Scriptures, and book). More questions are provided than you will have time to cover; select in advance those questions you would like to discuss, putting a checkmark beside each one.

The Video

Play: Session 4: God Is Faithful (running time: 17:50)

Discuss:

- What is the difference between a covenant and a contract? *(If not discussed as a conversation starter)*
- Why is it so important to understand that God made a covenant with his people, not a contract?

- How is Christmas a fulfillment of God's covenant?
- How is the manger connected to the cross?
- What is the message of the cross? What does it mean for our lives?
- What did God do when the Law and the prophets did not change our hearts? Why did he take this action?
- How can we come to trust God's faithfulness more?

The Book

In Chapter 4, we read about a God who is completely faithful and true. God is a covenant God who keeps his covenant even when we stray from it. God is a God who steps into our lives to save us, redeem us, and show us what a life with him looks like.

Discuss:

- In what ways do we sometimes treat the covenants we make like contracts?
- In the section "An Unlikely Love Story," how is the overarching story of the Old Testament described? How is this our story too?
- Discuss the idea that Christmas is about God demonstrating faithfulness. In what ways is Christmas a demonstration of God's faithfulness?
- What was the price of God's faithfulness?

- What should we do with our struggles, our pain, our doubts, our questions, and even our sin? What has God promised when we come to him with these things?

Bible Study

In Advance: Use a commentary or Bible dictionary as needed to help you prepare for this segment. Choose one or more of the following texts (depending upon time available and your group dynamics and needs). Be familiar with the text before the group session begins. Write down your own discussion questions in addition to those provided below.

Read Aloud: Isaiah 42:6-7

Discuss:

- What covenant is God making with his people?
- What does God promise?
- What will God's people do as a result of living out their side of the covenant?

Read Aloud: Galatians 4:4-5

Discuss:

- Who does this passage include in the promises of God?
- What does it mean to be adopted into God's family?

- How should we live in response to this great act of God's love?

Read Aloud: Isaiah 49:8-11, 13, 15-16

Discuss:

- Name the promises of God in these verses.
- How do you respond to the idea that you are engraved on the palms of God's hands?
- What does it mean to you this Advent that God is faithful—always and forever?

Conclude by reading 1 John 3:1 aloud. Remind participants that we are children of a loving, faithful God. We can come to him with everything we have been, everything we are, and everything we want to be; and he has promised to love us and to be for us. What a promise to savor!

Life Application

Say:

As our Advent study draws to a close, let's consider the gift that awaits us and the gifts we are eager to give. More importantly, let's consider the gift we have in Jesus and the gifts we give to him when we lay ourselves at his feet.

On a piece of paper, draw two packages. Label the first one "From Jesus" and the second one "To Jesus." Inside the gift labeled "From Jesus," list the ways that Jesus is a gift in your life. Recall some ways you have experienced his love and his faithfulness time and time again. Then, inside the gift labeled "To Jesus," make a list of the ways in which you can live your life in response to Jesus' gift, letting your whole life be a gift to Jesus.

Chapter 4 closes with these promises: "You can trust our God because he is a covenant God. Our God is a for-better-or-for-worse kind of God. Our God is a till-death-do-us-part kind of God—and even *then* he's an I'm-not-through-loving-you kind of God. He will not forget you. How could he? Your name is engraved on the palms of his hands. Our God is forever and always faithful."

As you remember the ways God has been a gift in your life, remember to invite God to give you awareness of those people in your life who do not know Jesus. Pray for these people and for the courage to invite them to church or to tell them the story of Jesus.

Closing (10 Minutes)

A Final Reflection

Say:

God's faithfulness is proven from the manger to the cross to the empty tomb. You can trust him; he is faithful. This Christmas, may we all receive anew the gift of Jesus in our lives and renew our commitment to live in relationship with our faithful, covenant God.

Closing Prayer

Faithful God, you are wonderful. You truly are a gift to us, and we are grateful for who you are and all you've done. Strengthen us to live out our covenant with you. Embolden us to live in response to your faithfulness, trusting that you are a God who will do what you say you will do. Thank you for the Christ child in the manger. Thank you for stepping into our lives. Receive our hearts as a gift in response to your great love for us. Amen.

CHRISTMAS SESSION

A Season of Joy

Christmas Session
A Season of Joy

Preparation

Session Objective

Participants will explore the joy of Jesus.

Main Themes

- God came to earth wrapped up in Jesus.
- Rejoicing is a fitting way to celebrate Jesus' birth.
- We can run home to God.

Key Scripture

Glory to God in the heavenly heights,
Peace to all men and women on earth who please him.

Luke 2:14 THE MESSAGE

Materials Needed

You will need the *Under Wraps DVD*, a DVD player, and a Bible.

Getting Started (10 Minutes)

Opening Prayer

Amazing God, we are overjoyed that you came to earth wrapped up in swaddling clothes. You came into our world to live among us and to love us, redeem us, and claim us. Thank you for your awesome gift. Amen.

Conversation Starter

Say:

The final word we come to at Christmas is *joy*. Because of who God is, because of all God has done, we can have joy in every circumstance life throws at us. This is a season of joy because God has fulfilled his covenant to rescue us. We close *Under Wraps* with joy as we finally get to unwrap the gift: God's gift of Jesus.

Ask:

Choose one of the following:

- How do you experience joy during the Christmas season?

- What are your favorite Christmas carols that you love to sing to God?

Video, Discussion, and Application (30 Minutes)

Note: This section allows approximately 25 minutes total for discussion (of video, Scriptures, and book). More questions are provided than you will have time to cover; select in advance those questions you would like to discuss, putting a checkmark beside each one.

The Video

Play: Epilogue: A Season of Joy (running time: 4:42)

Discuss:

- What are some descriptive words for the Christmas season? *(Have participants call them out as you list them on a board or chart.)*
- How does the idea that Christmas is about God getting his kids back expand your view of the Christmas celebration?
- How is joy the culmination of all of our Christmas experiences?

Bible Study

In Advance: Use a commentary or Bible dictionary as needed to help you prepare for this segment. Choose one or more of the following texts (depending upon time available and your group dynamics and needs). Be familiar with the text before the group session begins. Write down your own discussion questions in addition to those provided below.

Read Aloud: Luke 15: 20-24

Discuss:

- How does the parable of the lost son help us understand God's joy as he gives the gift of himself wrapped up in Jesus?
- How would you describe the father's joy in the parable?
- How do you think God reacts when we come home to him?

Read Aloud: Luke 2:8-14

Discuss:

- Which verses in this passage tell us something about joy? What do they tell us?
- The gift of Jesus was announced to shepherds by choirs of angels. How can we celebrate with the angel choir this Christmas?

Conclude with these words from the epilogue: "Hallelujah! What a Savior! Because of God's great gift to us—God himself, wrapped up in Jesus—we can rejoice at Christmastime at his great love for us. We can be free to unwrap God's great gift with unabashed joy and wonder and celebration, eager to show off the wonderful gift he has given. We can run to the Father, whose arms are open wide, welcoming us home. We can heartily sing, 'Joy to the world! The Lord is come!'"

Life Application

Say:

As we sum up our journey, let's consider the new discoveries, learnings, and challenges we've experienced.

How has "unwrapping" God in Jesus enriched your preparation for Christmas this Advent season? What can you do to share your wonder, excitement, and joy for God's wonderful gift with others?

Closing (5 Minutes)

A Final Reflection

Say:

Through Jesus Christ, God revealed to us who he was and is. Through Jesus, we are able to joyfully receive the wonderful gift of God's love and mercy, which he is pleased to give to us.

If your group is willing, close your session by singing together "Joy to the World." If yours is not a group of singers, read aloud this passage from The Message Bible:

There were sheepherders camping in the neighborhood. They had set night watches over their sheep. Suddenly, God's angel stood among them and God's glory blazed around them. They were terrified. The angel said, "Don't be afraid. I'm here to announce a great and joyful event that is meant for everybody, worldwide: A Savior has just been born in David's town, a Savior who is Messiah and Master. This is what you're to look for: a baby wrapped in a blanket and lying in a manger."

At once the angel was joined by a huge angelic choir singing God's praises:

> *Glory to God in the heavenly heights,*
> *Peace to all men and women on earth who please him.*
> Luke 2:8-14 THE MESSAGE

Closing Prayer

What a gift you have given to us, O God. You have entered our world wrapped up in Jesus Christ and have come to rescue your beloved children. Thank you for the joy and the wonder of it all. Help us to live with joy as your children—claimed, redeemed, and freed to live an abundant life. Give us the voice to tell the whole world that you have come and that you are Love. Amen.